SAM FEENEY'S

CAREER FACTORS

Unlock fulfilling work…
without leaving your job.

Sam Feeney
Foreword by Dr. Bryan Hendley

SAM FEENEY'S CAREER FACTORS

Unlock Fulfilling Work ... Without Leaving Your Job

Second Edition of
The Career Factors

ISBN 979-8-9881279-8-7

Emissary

Published in Phoenix, Arizona by Emissary Publishing.
Emissary is a business trade name of Ed's Voices, LLC.

DEDICATION

To anyone who wants more from their career
than just a paycheck.
Although those are nice, too.

CONTENTS

Sam Feeney's Career Factors

FOREWORD

While I have been privileged to engage with Sam on this project, collaborating with him on the coaching process associated with The Career Factors and serving as a guinea pig for the different iterations of the assessment, I am especially humbled and honored to write the foreword for this book.

Diving into The Career Factors with Sam has been an eye-opening experience for me, and one that led to great reflection on my own career journey. If you are anything like me (and statistically in the majority), your career journey has not been linear. There have been twists and unexpected turns. There have been jobs you never thought you would have, roles you never thought you'd enjoy, and positions you thought you'd love that turned out to be less than what you'd hoped for. You likely have a degree in one area and are now working in something (seemingly) unrelated, at least directly. My career, and likely yours, has been so intertwined with my life, and in the past, I found myself frustrated with one aspect or another of my job, often unable to put my finger on it, other than to know that something was "off".

The Career Factors allowed me to put a name to what had previously been just out of reach for me. The process allowed me a deeper understanding of what I had been looking for in my work, and in some ways, in my life. Perhaps my favorite and most impactful piece of The Career Factors is the belief that career satisfaction is an inside job.

Wow! As Sam points out, the natural inclination is to argue back, to start the "yeah, buts…", and to place the burden on the organizations with whom we work for our fulfillment in our careers. Instead, Sam challenges us to take this responsibility on for ourselves, and not only that, but he provides us with the tools and encouragement to take that challenge head on.

There is great power for us here in this choice. We have the opportunity to learn what it is we truly want to get out of our careers, determine how we can apply that in our current situation, and then take action on our Career Factors in order to create work that is meaningful, fulfilling, and supportive of our gifts and talents.

One final encouragement from me:

Our careers don't have to satisfy our every need, and when we look for them to do so, we'll likely be disappointed. While some folks may find their "dream job", others can work in places and positions that they find fulfilling, meaningful, and important, that may not, from the outside, fall into that "dream job" category. And that's just fine! In fact, that's more of the norm. We can create meaningful work, right where we are.

As you continue to seek to create fulfilling work—right where you are (wherever you are)—I'm pulling for you.

Bryan

Bryan Hendley, Ed D.
Creator of The Purpose Project

A NOTE TO THE READER

This book is designed to be somewhat interactive, featuring free assessments drawn from our coaching program. To access your free resources and learn more about using the Career Factors to unlock fulfilling work in your current role, visit thecareerfactors.com.

Each chapter of the book begins with the ongoing story of a fictional character we'll call Marcus. Stories are the best teachers, and this book presents a fair amount of new information—or at least new ways of looking at something very familiar—so I hope that including a story that weaves the chapters together will help you understand the concepts and how you can apply them to your own career journey.

Part 1 is a review of traditional career development, with some important shifts in the mindset around career satisfaction that will prove useful as you understand how you got to wherever you are in your career.

If you'd prefer to jump to how to apply your Career Factors to your current job without the walk down memory lane and the argument for doing careers differently, feel free to take the free assessment at thecareerfactors.com and learn how to use your results in Part 2.

INTRODUCTION

Why Work Matters

It is impossible to have a great life unless it is a meaningful life. And it is very difficult to have a meaningful life without meaningful work.
– Jim Collins

---

thecareerfactors.com

Do you remember your first day of work? Maybe like me you had a job in high school working after school or on the weekends so you could buy things you wanted. Fast forward a bit to your first real job, the one you prepared for with college or trade school or an apprenticeship. Think back for a minute to your first day at that job. What were you feeling? Was it excitement at finally being able to do what you had been dreaming about for years? Was it nervousness at the wave of unknowns that faced you? Was it disappointment because of the other jobs you applied for but didn't get?

Whatever you felt on your first day of work, how does it compare to your feelings about work today? What are your expectations of work as you begin each day? What do you hope to get from your career as you look into the future?

The Weight of Work

For many people, work falls into one of two general categories: calling or curse. Some people truly come alive when they work, gladly giving their all to a career that seems to be a higher calling. You might marvel at their energy and their attitude as they discuss the time and effort they invest into their jobs. For others, work is a necessary evil, a cross to bear for 40 hours a week with no real redeeming value. Every mention of work becomes a seeming contest to prove how much worse their job is than someone else's in a game that no one wins.

No matter which end of the continuum you tend toward, there is no denying that our work affects our lives beyond providing for our physical needs. Just by the sheer volume of time it demands, your job bleeds into every other area of your life, and it is important to recognize those effects.

Your identity: Like it or not, who we are is in large part defined by what we do for work. Which makes sense if you think about it: the function of most things in our lives is the basis of its identity. Computers began as computation machines, automobiles travel from one place to another (without the aid of horses), and our planners keep us on task throughout the day. Ask anyone with the last name Cooper, Baker, or Smith, and they'll agree that what you do can define you.

Further, we're wired to put people in boxes as a way to make sense of the world, so the second question we ask anyone we meet (after, "What did he say your name is?") is "What do you do?" Which is all well and good unless a.) you aren't "doing" anything at the moment because you're between jobs or b.) you're unhappy with your career. But that's our oversimplifying default: identity based on function.

Your family: If we are in fact "the average of the five people we spend the most time with," as business philosopher Jim Rohn attested, then who you work with is rubbing off on your family. While you may not bring your co-workers home to dinner with you, your constant interactions with them influence your interactions with your family, whether you're still processing a conflict with a supervisor while your daughter shares about her day at school or you're on a high after a big contract is secured while your spouse unloads on you about a home project you've been neglecting.

Your pace of life: We are creatures of rhythms, patterns, and habits, so our jobs can dramatically affect our habits, especially over time. Compare the working life of someone who works in accounts payable for a mid-sized company to that of an elementary teacher. The former has a job that is by no means easy, but is likely fairly predictable, allowing him to create routines that allow for clear transitions between work and life. On the other hand, the second-grade teacher's life is one largely of controlled chaos—no matter how well a lesson has been planned—as the needs and demands of 26 seven-year-olds consume the teacher's attention until dismissal, leaving her to scramble from school to home, finishing plans for the next day after everyone else in the house is asleep. And tomorrow will be the same...

Sometimes we're so close to a problem and it has become so normalized that we don't see it until someone holds up a mirror to our lives. Clayton Christensen, the late Harvard MBA professor, gives us two pictures of how work affects us as he observed a member of his team at a company picnic with her family:

[Diana] wasn't just a scientist. She was a mother and a wife, whose mood, whose happiness, and whose sense of self-worth had a huge impact on her family. What must it be like in her house in the morning, as she said good-by to her family on her way to work? I saw Diana in my mind's eye as she came home to her family ten hours later, on a day that had gone badly. She felt underappreciated, frustrated, and demeaned; she learned little that was new. In that moment I... saw how her day at work negatively affected the way she interacted in the evening with her husband and their young children.

This vision in my mind then fast-forwarded to the end of another day. On the one hand, she was so engaged by the experiment she was doing that she wanted to stay at work; but on the other, she was so looking forward to spending time with her husband and children that she clearly wanted to be at home. On that day, I saw her driving home with greater self-esteem – feeling that she had learned a lot, having been recognized in a positive way for achieving valuable things, and played a significant role in the success of some important initiatives for several scientists and for the company. I... could see her go into her home at the end of the day with a replenished reservoir of esteem that profoundly affected her interaction with her husband and those two lovely children. And I also knew how she'd feel going into work the next day – motivated and energized (*How Will You Measure Your Life*, p. 26-27) .

Which picture best describes your current work experience? You can take the Career Factors Check-in diagnostic at thecareerfactors.com to find out.

CHAPTER 1

An Antiquated Approach
**The outdated way we chose our careers...
and how that limits us today**

We cannot solve our
problems with the same
thinking we used when
we created them.
– Albert Einstein

___

thecareerfactors.com

Marcus poked his head into his school counselor's office to see if any other students were there before entering.

"You wanted to see me, Mrs. R?"

"Yes, Marcus, come on in," Mrs. Rydell answered, not looking up from her computer. "Just finishing something up."

Marcus sat in the lone seat across the desk from Mrs. Rydell and waited for her to look up. He knew that they were going to talk about picking classes for next year—*senior year*—and he hoped she had more of a plan than he did.

"Thanks for waiting, Marcus. I asked you to come down so we can pick your courses for next year. Senior year—pretty exciting!"

Marcus just nodded and smiled politely.

"Before we begin, what are your plans for after graduation? Will you be going to college?"

Marcus knew this question was coming, but he didn't have a good answer. Yes? Probably? What else was he supposed to do?

Mrs. Rydell continued, "Your grades are strong, especially if you want to go to any of the state schools. And I see that you've done well in Biology and Chemistry. Maybe you could go pre-med."

"Yeah… maybe," was all that Marcus offered.
"Is everything okay, Marcus?" Mrs. Rydell asked, sitting back in her chair and closing her laptop.

After a moment, Marcus replied, "I'm good, Mrs. R. It's just that I really have no idea what I want to do after high school. My mom went to college but hates her job, and my stepdad keeps telling me that I should go because he regrets not going. That it will be the best thing for me to get ahead in life. I really love sports, but I know I'm not going pro, so I'm not sure what else to do."

Mrs. Rydell leaned forward and gave a warm, understanding smile.

"I know how you feel, Marcus. And it's okay. Many of your classmates feel the same way at this time in their lives. Graduating from high school is a big step, and you'll make some important decisions in the next year and a half that will shape your future. I know that you'll choose the right path for you.

"You mentioned sports; what about a career in sports medicine? You could be a trainer like Miss Render or maybe even a surgeon for a sports team!"

Marcus left the meeting with his school counselor encouraged by her belief in him but still without any clear direction for what he should do after high school. College seemed the logical choice, but what did he know about being a doctor or a trainer? You have to admit, he thought, it would be pretty cool to be on the sidelines for a big-time football game or help a Hall of

Famer get back on the mound after an injury. And pre-med certainly sounds pretty cool if anyone asks what I'm doing after high school...

Our earliest impressions of work—both what we saw around us and what we saw for ourselves—have a lasting effect on the career we chose, our decisions about making changes along our journey, and our satisfaction with our current role. Unfortunately, for many of us the messages we received about work and about our place in the working world have given us a faulty understanding of what it means to work and how to create a meaningful career. The collection of flawed premises that likely influenced (and still influence!) your career choices are not uncommon; in fact, many young people still operate under them today. But doing something wrong expertly does not eventually create the outcome you desire.

In this chapter we'll examine each outdated way of choosing a career, allowing you the opportunity to reflect on your journey and end with a very brief measure of the outcome. In other words, did the old way of choosing a career, making career decisions, and finding job satisfaction work for you?

The Big Four

Do you remember how you chose your career? Or perhaps how your career was chosen for you? Research tells us that the three primary influences on an individual's career choice are school, family, and society. Let's visit each one at a time.

School

Tell me if this sounds familiar: you meet with your school counselor (but he was called a guidance counselor then, right?) to choose your courses for the next year or to discuss the college application process. The counselor mentions that you seem to be doing well in Math, so you should be an engineer. Or you're doing well in Social Studies, so you might want to consider law. Or maybe you're not doing very well at all, so have you considered a trade school?

If you're like most people, one of your first exposures to career development in school was skills-based, the belief that your aptitudes determine your career path. When you think about it, school influence on students' careers is a self-perpetuating process, where you advance in subjects that initially come easily to you, thereby increasing your skills and scaffolding you to higher and higher levels. Meanwhile, the areas where you don't experience immediate success are minimized and dismissed, understood to be necessary evils. In essence, by focusing on areas of natural aptitude early in one's academic career, a career direction begins to form that at the same time excludes other areas based purely on innate skill.

Which isn't necessarily a bad thing because at least you have a direction! Woe to the student who has a B or C in everything and doesn't find any subject in school particularly engaging, especially as a career. How is an overworked and under-resourced school counselor supposed to help the student who has no obvious career path? Many students receive the advice to go to college and figure it out there; at least having a college degree will increase your chances at employment. The can is only kicked so far down the road. (Note: no shame to school counselors here. I was one! The Career Factors was born of necessity. Check out thecareerfactors.com for high school and college career guidance resources.)

Family

Just as important to a young person when choosing a career is the acceptance that is felt by one's family. Right or wrong, many of us considered or reacted to our families when making career decisions. For some, family and school seemed to be a collaboration, especially if our parents did well in school and were rewarded by following the advice of the school system; our parents relied on teachers and counselors to provide career direction.

Some middle-aged employees might recall choosing their careers based on approval, whether seeking to gain it by following the path suggested—or planned—for them or attempting to spurn them by heading down a completely different road. If you've read *The Great Gatsby*, you may recall the narrator Nick Carroway getting approval from his family to move to New York and enter the stock business… after he had graduated from Yale and fought in World War I! The desire to gain approval from our family can follow us for decades.

When a five-year-old is asked about her career aspirations and responds with, "I want to be an artist!" (or a firetruck or Kitty Fairy from *Gabby's Dollhouse*) , she's met with smiles and fawning approbation. Fast forward ten years, and that same desire to be a painter might elicit a thin smile or "That's nice," and soon after a relative asks for the first time, "How do you plan to make money doing that?" Come senior year of high school, it's time to get practical; after all, your brother is already living in the basement. "It's nice to have dreams, dear, but you need to choose a career where you can actually make money. Hey, maybe you can minor in art in college!"

Society

While school and family might offer more overt input for our career decisions, society's influence is a bit more insidious, and its impact is felt only as a person gains self-awareness. As I recall my own career journey, I knew—but likely would not have acknowledged or said out loud—that there were certain jobs that were out of my reach and other jobs that were seemingly beneath me based purely on my sixteen-year-old sense of status, where I fit in the tiny world I inhabited. In a sense, my career would mirror my place in society.

Where you were born and the environment you were raised in greatly affected you and your career decision simply by what you were exposed to—and what you weren't—including work experiences and role models. The messages you might receive about your career options and the value of work (and work ethic) are

7

dramatically different if you grew up in Appalachia or if you grew up in Palo Alto.

Trends in the Job Market

The final external career influence is rooted in something as simple as when you were born. Trends in the job market you anticipate entering may have played a part in your choice of career. For example, you might use an expected surge of health care jobs for a retiring generation as a reason to enter geriatrics. Or you might initially explore a career in commercial real estate only to be talked out of it by statistics about online shopping and remote work.

I want to be clear: these external influences are not in and of themselves bad or wrong. They're just external both in origin **and** in destination, creating an outcome-dependent sense of career selection that can follow you for decades. So, what's the remedy? For one, opting for career direction over career selection.

Career Direction > Career Selection

One of the inherent flaws in how you likely chose your career was that it was outcome-based, meaning your career was a point to be reached, not a journey begin. Put another way, career selection was valued over career direction. This is covered in greater detail in *The Career Factors for Students*, but it's important for our conversation in chapter four, so I'll quickly summarize here.

In its simplest terms, career selection is just that: choosing a career. At the surface, there's nothing wrong with that; after all, shouldn't that be the desire of any young person? However, in my years of working with young people, attempts to help them choose a career often created more anxiety and resistance than excitement and anticipation. Why was career selection problematic?

One of the problems with career selection was the definiteness of it. Juniors who are faced with choosing a career feel the weight of **commitment** that accompanies it, especially if they are going to invest time and money (or already have!) in an educational program before beginning that career. While those of us who have been in the workforce for a few years recognize the opportunities to pivot and transition throughout one's career, the question of career selection may feel like it requires a forty-year answer. Ironically, once someone begins the career they've chosen—having attained the desired goal—there's a tendency to settle or atrophy since getting the job was the target.

Big decisions also bring the pressure of **getting it right**, so guiding young people to choose a specific career unwittingly favors a list of predictable careers that either sound impressive or are readily understood. Think of it this way: if you were asked to choose one stock that would make up your entire retirement portfolio, would you bet on the hottest company in an emerging market or a tried-and-true blue chip? While they can't put those words to it many young people (and former young people like you and me) choose careers that have the greatest likelihood of measurable success. Which isn't a bad thing in and of itself, unless that's not the right career for you.

The last challenge that a forced-choice approach to career development presents is that it's **time-sensitive**. Actually, there are two challenges when there's a clock running on your choice. First, there is a tendency to make the easiest choice, the one that will create the fewest ripples or that seems most logical to those around you. Second, a finite selection can only be made from the available options, whether that's the jobs that currently exist or the jobs that you're aware of from your current vantage point. (More on both of those in a minute.)

All of this may sound rather reasonable to some readers, especially since it's what we've known for the past century. And if it worked for you— you enjoyed your career selection process and you're in a career you love—that's great! However, I quickly propose an alternative, not only for today's students, but for those of us who might have felt the weight of a time-bound, outcome-based career development experience: career direction.

Career direction is the belief that—while the destination is important—the journey matters more, that one's choices and motivations will evolve over time and that a career should be just as malleable and responsive. Consider the westward explorers who first mapped our country; while many of them had a particular destination in mind (and some even reached it!) , their greater contribution to posterity was charting the expanse between what was known and what was not yet discovered. If your family plans a vacation to Cocoa Beach but is thwarted by a late-season hurricane, the fun is ruined; if instead you point the car generally Southeast, hundreds of options for a memorable time together await.

Career direction is different than career selection in at least three ways, *even if the eventual job description is the same*:

1. **Commitment:** The commitment we make is to begin the journey, but not that it will end at a particular point. In this we value each step for itself, learning more about the steps we've taken and about what we really want.

2. **Outcome:** If—as sometimes happens—life gets in the way of your career selection and you never reach it or you take longer that you "should have", regret for what might have been can anchor one's mind to a time that cannot be reclaimed. However, career direction recognizes that there are many points along the way, each a possible stopping point, whether for a season or altogether.

3. **Time pressure:** The realist is quick to pipe up here and note that, yes, students do eventually have to make a decision! You can't kick the can down the road forever. However, career direction shifts the question from "What do you want to do after you graduate?" (bringing with it all the weight of choosing a 40-year career) to "What do you want to do *next?*" You should see the relief that crosses

students' faces when you ask that question. You may have even felt a little lighter as you read that.

Career direction isn't just for young people; it's a new way to look at career that gives you and me the freedom to explore and rediscover what we want our careers to look like... and to help others do the same.

The Exception

For some, the preceding discussion might not apply; instead, choosing a career was an internally driven process, often beginning at a very young age. However, some in this group of outliers experienced resistance from the career influences we examined and continued pursuing their aspirations in spite of the external forces seemingly allied against them.

Conclusion

Is there anything inherently wrong with these career influences? Is it a bad thing that school, our families, and society have so greatly impacted our career decisions? I propose that for many of us there is something wrong with the way we chose our careers. Two main problems appear:

1. There's a tendency to make decisions about career based on two major criteria: skills and security.

2. All three influences—school, family, and society—are external influences.

We'll take the next two chapters to unpack each.

Reflection: What were the main career influences in choosing your career? What are your main career influences now? What messages did you receive about work when you were growing up? Which of those do you still hold to?

CHAPTER 2

A More Elegant Problem:
Understanding what really motivates us at work… by learning about what doesn't

"People may spend their whole lives climbing the ladder of success only to find, once they reach the top, that the ladder is leaning against the wrong wall."
- Thomas Merton

———

thecareerfactors.com

Marcus lay awake, staring at the ceiling. His phone read 2:18AM. Jacqui stirred next to him, but she was a heavy sleeper; she wouldn't notice that he couldn't sleep. Again.

He ran back through the last few days, trying to figure out what had set him off. Things were pretty stressful at work right now, especially since the team had made the playoffs and the training staff was working two seasons at the same time. The frenetic pace that had once been so exciting was now a strain. On his marriage. On his relationship with his kids.

His afternoon with Kyra was supposed to be a daddy-daughter date, but he ended up snapping at her for being on her phone and snapping at the waiter for taking too long with the appetizers and snapping in his head at pretty much everyone and everything else for the rest of the day.

He wasn't usually like this. What was wrong?

Marcus arrived at work at his normal time, which was early for everyone else. He had always prided himself in being early. But today he was understandably sluggish, which Randal picked up on right away.

"Hey, Marcus. You look like a hundred bucks. You okay?"

Marcus acknowledged Randal's assessment with a grim smile. "Yeah, I'm good. Just couldn't sleep last night."

"No fun, man. Everything okay at home?"

"Everything's fine. I just had a rough weekend with the fam."

Randal let the comment hang in the air, waiting to see if Marcus would elaborate.

"I got mad at Kyra for no real reason and then was mad for pretty much the entire weekend. And I can't figure out why."

"Hey, man. This is a really stressful time at work. I get it."

"But work is work. And we have it really good here: good money, a ton of perks, and our equipment is brand new. I landed my dream job, but it doesn't feel like a dream for some reason. I know I should be happy here, but I'm really not.

Um... don't tell anyone I said that, okay?"

Randal smiled. "No worries, Marcus. You're not the only one who feels that way. Heck, I used to hate my job, and I brought that home with me. But I started changing the way I thought about it. And everything else changed, too."

Once we chose our initial careers, we felt a sense of accomplishment at having checked this gigantic, existential box and set out to do whatever it was that needed to be done for that job.

But for some of us, a sneaky thought began to nibble at the edges of our understanding of what a job is: Do I enjoy this work?

Enter the sometimes rough and seemingly uncharted seas of career satisfaction, the sense of satisfaction you derive from not only your current role, but the direction it seems to be heading. Employers work hard to improve their employees' job satisfaction, and employees want to be happy in their jobs. But often both parties end up frustrated. The employee complains; the employer gets defensive; they stick it out like a bad marriage until one of them calls it quits.

Why?

As we discovered in the previous chapter, the process many of us used to choose our careers created an externally-based understanding of what is required to be satisfied with our jobs. In fact, we were conditioned—and in a way conditioned ourselves—to take an external approach to job satisfaction because of how we chose our jobs. After all, if the reasons I chose my job were external, wouldn't the measures of whether my career is going well tend to be external also? Wouldn't I use the same measuring stick; in fact, the only one I have at hand?

The early research on psychology and motivation demonstrated the power of external effects of motivation, influenced famously by pioneers like Pavlov and Skinner, who broke ground in the field with experiments that demonstrated the impact of external stimulus on behavior. And we behave in a way that gets a direct, related result. Right? As it turns out, *kind of*. We're a bit more complicated than that. More on this later.

Research regarding employee satisfaction focused first on what was called incentive (or principal-agent) theory, the idea being that if employees had incentives, they would behave in a way that got them closer to those incentives and—once reached—would experience higher levels of job satisfaction. Which used to be called *survival*. Remember that the idea of job satisfaction is a relatively new one. Work has changed dramatically in the past two centuries, initially having only one desired outcome: staying warm, dry, and fed. The resultant attitude about work? It's work; be happy you have it. That attitude has been handed down to many of us and is a hard one to shake.

However, as the effects of improved technology and increased population changed America's workforce, employers who wanted to engage their employees in a competitive market began introducing incentives. According to researchers Jensen and Meckling, the best ways to motivate employees include

- Status – the position within the company and how it's seen by peers and supervisors
- Compensation – a proper return for the value given
- Job security – the expectation of future employment based on current performance
- Work conditions – where and how you work
- Company policies – how the company operates

- Supervisory practices – the feedback loop for employees

Not a bad list! On the surface, if your expectations were met or exceeded in all of these areas, you'd be pretty happy with your job, right?

Turns out—surprisingly—no. While external motivators aren't in and of themselves bad, they aren't great at keeping people happy at their jobs. But why?

One clue is in another name for external motivators: hygiene factors. Who gets excited about hygiene... or even notices it? Until it's not there. The presence of these factors wouldn't make you happy with your job; it just wouldn't make you *unhappy*. According to Harvard MBA professor Clayton Christensen's book *How Will You Measure Your Life*, "If you instantly improve the hygiene factors of your job, you're not going to suddenly love it. At best, you just won't *hate* it anymore. The opposite of *job dissatisfaction* isn't *job satisfaction*, but rather an *absence of job dissatisfaction*." (33)

When an employee considers the characteristics of hygiene factors, he or she begins to see how minimally satisfying these motivators can be, even though they're all that most of us were taught to look for in a career.

For one, hygiene factors are largely circumstantial, byproducts of a variety of influences including government policy, location, economic cycles, and industry trends. To the average employees, these are tides against which it's easier to go with than to fight. As these are all outside of one's control, relying on them also leaves an employee at the whim of these forces, resulting in no agency to improve career satisfaction. It's similar to a farmer who plants his crop and is forced to wait for rain (and pray for no locusts) in order to see whether he'll have a harvest in the fall.

Another shortcoming of an externally focused career satisfaction model is that it becomes comparative, reducing the value of not only others but oneself to compensation, status, etc. This is obviously a flawed perspective, but without naming it, it becomes normalized. So it makes sense when someone complains about the bonuses someone at another company received or when another person feels a sense of superiority about a promotion. But that behavior is actually pretty childish, like the kid who wants a new toy just because everyone else has it or who lords their newfound status as line leader over their classmates, only to discover a few days later that the role has lost its luster.

Career motivation that is external can also be quite reductionist. If you're familiar with Maslow's Hierarchy of Needs, you might recall that the lowest levels are safety and physiological needs, those that are tied to how much we get paid at our jobs. Does getting more compensation move us to higher levels of existence by meeting more needs? No. We just get to be safer and have more of our physiological needs met. Nothing wrong with that, but those factors won't bring happiness. Instead, they keep us at the lower levels of existence.

Unfortunately, the reductionist nature of externally motivated career satisfaction also shows up in how we treat each other. It's not uncommon for birds of a feather to flock together within a corporate setting, and the primary ways of segmenting a company are compensation and status. Instead of bringing people together behind a compelling mission, many companies unwittingly promote transactional working relationships that minimize much of who a person is, effectively making them cogs in a wheel. This is a justifiable practice because the bottom line is the bottom line, but when this tendency rubs off on us and how we treat others, we end up missing out on transformational relationships with some really amazing people because we've been conditioned to esteem them based on our external lenses.

Not only does career satisfaction that is purely external eventually pit us against each other, it doesn't create lasting satisfaction. Christensen continues, "Compensation is a hygiene factor. You need to get it right. But all you can aspire to is that employees will not be mad at each other and the company because of compensation" (33). Remember, this kind of career satisfaction just keeps dissatisfaction at bay. When the bonuses dry up and you run out of rungs to climb on the corporate ladder, what are you left with?

I'm not saying for a moment that how much you get paid is unimportant; I have declined interviews for jobs once I determined how much the position paid, and my family loves being able to live indoors with the money I make. However, focusing on it as a motivator for career satisfaction rather than as a reward for a job well done eventually commoditizes the position and even (especially in the eyes of a company) yourself. Instead, "we should always remember that beyond a certain point, hygiene factors such as money, status, compensation, and job security are much more a by-product of being happy with a job rather than the cause of it. Realizing this frees us to focus on the things that really matter" (40) .

While some of you are tracking with me, others are potentially resisting the implications of my argument for something more effective than externally derived career motivation. After all, you might say, it's what we've always done. Why try to change it? Aren't there benefits to operating this way? Otherwise, why would we have started doing it in the first place? To which I reply: absolutely.

If you rely on external motivators to inform your career decisions, including which career to pursue, whether to take a promotion, or when to change companies, you operate in an outcome-based—almost binary—space that allows you to make complicated variables much simpler. Does it pay more? Do I get a better lifestyle because of it? Does it fit my skill set? If those boxes get checked, then it's all systems go. This approach is also great for someone who is analytical because it's easier to understand and to justify. Quantifiability can bring confidence because as the saying goes, "What you can measure, you treasure."

But what happens once you take that job? Does it bring you the satisfaction you're looking for, or do you start looking for a job that pays more or provides more status or has better perks six months later?

If that sounds familiar, it may be because the anticipation of something new can be so powerful. The excitement of chasing the brass ring is undeniable, but what happens when as your career progresses (and you age) the opportunities to get a raise—or the amount of the raises themselves—lessen? Like a getting a new toy at Christmas, the anticipation of achievement might have been more appealing to us than actually attaining it.

Another reason the rat race is so called has to do with what psychologists call stimulus satiation, a phenomenon where we become demotivated by what once appealed to us. Remember Pavlov's dog? The initial excitement of stimulus-response gets us moving toward a raise or promotion, but what happens once we get it? Often, what drew us to a particular job fades, and we're left with a sense of dissatisfaction or boredom with our compensation or duties. Having known a number of people with highly paid careers, I've observed a heightened level of discontent as they neared the end of their careers, almost as if they're asking, "Was the money worth all I had to do—and give up—to make it?"

The effect of relying on these external motivators to bring us true career satisfaction aren't in and of themselves bad; they're just limited. At some point in time, they will fall short of giving you everything you need. And that brass ring becomes golden handcuffs, making you feel trapped in a job that no longer makes you happy… even though the money is great.

CHAPTER 3

Plumbing the Depths:
Uncovering the internal career motivators

The problem is that what we think matters most in our jobs does not align with what will really make us happy.
– Clayton Christensen

—

thecareerfactors.com

Marcus muddled through the next few months, more or less ignoring the gnawing feeling in his gut that something wasn't as it should be. But on the second day of a long-anticipated vacation Jacqui asked him the $64,000 question.

"Marcus, what's wrong?"

"Wrong? Nothing. I'm sitting here on the beach with you watching Kyra play in the waves. I am A-OK."

"And I love that we get to be here. But it seems like something's bothering you. Even with your toes in the sand, something's on your mind."

"That obvious, huh?"

"Yeah. And it's been weighing on you for months. Kyra and I are on eggshells around you, trying not to poke the bear."

Marcus was quiet for almost a minute, which seemed like an eternity for both of them.

"I don't know, baby. I just hate my job. It sounds so stupid when I say it out loud. I mean, who doesn't? Aren't you supposed to hate your job? Isn't that what makes *Office Space* so funny?"

Jacqui looked surprised, which made Marcus feel even worse.

"I'm sorry, honey. I didn't know you felt that way." But she had nothing else to offer.

Marcus waited a moment and continued, "I know I should be happy. I know I should just suck it up and be grateful that I even have a job, let alone one that others would love to have. But I feel like it's sucking the life out of me. And I feel guilty for feeling like this."

"Have you talked to anyone at work about this?" Jacqui inquired. "Maybe you can work fewer hours or take the team lead they keep offering you. But whatever is bothering you, I hope you get it figured out soon because it's taking a toll on us."

Later that afternoon, Marcus created a note in his phone called **happy at work**. He started making a list of people he knew who loved their jobs, people who seemed like they'd won the job lottery. "What must it be like to get up every day and be excited about your work?" he thought. Had he ever felt that way?

Shane: Able to choose projects that make a difference in the causes that are important to him.

Monique: No matter how stressful work gets, she loves her co-workers and talks about them like her second family.

Corrie: With a hybrid remote schedule, she integrates her work into her life instead of her life into her work.

Manny: Uses work as his M.B.A. instead of going back to school. Always learning… and applying what he learns.

Marcus stepped back and reviewed his list. Where was the big salary, the company car, and the perks, all the incentives that had become so important to others in his industry? These four didn't care about those things, although two of them made great money.

Either they were wired differently, or Marcus had been missing some pieces of the puzzle...

As the workplace has evolved dramatically in the past century, so has our understanding of what motivates us at work. In response to the oversimplistic limits of Jensen and Meckling's incentive theory, which says that we are motivated primarily by external carrots and sticks, Frederick Herzberg began to offer the motivation—or two-factor—theory in the 1960s. He proposed that there are two continuums of job satisfaction: one that creates dissatisfaction and one that creates satisfaction. Put another way, there are certain things about our jobs that will make us unhappy, but *there are a separate set of factors that will make us happy.*

As you might guess, the external characteristics of one's career include status, salary, skills, and working conditions, all of which Herzberg called "hygiene factors." As we discussed in the last chapter, these are important, and for a long time, they were enough for a generation of workers who were thrilled to be rewarded for their labor by more than just survival. But even as those factors continued to increase in the post-World War II economic boom, the euphoria experienced by the now largely suburban workforce began to wane. Even with all that they had—and especially in comparison to their parents and Depression-era grandparents—they weren't happy. They were just less dissatisfied in a better zip code. In essence, Herzberg discovered that better pay, perks, and pensions cannot in and of themselves create career satisfaction!

If you'll allow me, I'm reminded of an episode of *The Fresh Prince of Bel-Air*, starring Will Smith. When Will wrestles with the hormones produced by unrequited love, his uncle Phil suggests a cold shower. Will dismisses the older man's suggestion with, "Come on, Uncle Phil, *this is the nineties!*" In the same way, what worked with the previous generation no longer works for us.

What, then, is missing, you and Marcus ask? What can bring me satisfaction in my career? Not to be too obvious, but Herzberg called them motivators. These motivating influences include challenging work, recognition, responsibility, and personal growth. Unlike the hygiene factors, these characteristics of work can create career satisfaction because they fit more closely who we are as humans, particularly in three important ways.

Motivators Are Intrinsic

If you've been a parent or perhaps a supervisor or coach, you know the challenge that's presented by trying to get someone to do something that he or she really doesn't feel like doing. Incentives quickly lose their power, and tactics like coercion and even threats can seem like the only tools that will work. I hope you've also experienced the excitement (or is it relief?) in figuring out how to make an externally motivated task become an internally motivated one, where the individual actually wants to do it!

Whether you're an employer or an employee, you can see the benefits of having challenging work, recognition, responsibility, and personal growth in the experience of work.

Motivators Are Self-determined

A more nuanced approach to job satisfaction also allows us to be more responsive to our growth and development as a person throughout our lives. Think back for a moment: what motivated you in your teens? How about in your twenties? If you're a little older, consider your primary reason for doing what you did in your thirties and forties. What matters to you as a person often changes in different seasons of life. Might that also be true of what you want from work?

A friend of mine, John, was a hard-charging vice president for a national bank who always scored at the highest levels on his annual reviews and consistently received increased compensation and responsibility at work. However, after he and his wife had twins, he chose to check his email less on the weekends and to be home for dinner most nights. During his next annual review, his supervisor reluctantly shared that he had received only satisfactory marks in some of the areas where he had previously excelled. John smiled and shared that he was okay with that because he was receiving higher scores at home than he ever had.

We'll discuss this more later, but one of the most intriguing characteristics of career satisfaction is that you and I can—at least in some ways—control it. No matter how abrasive your boss or how subpar your working conditions or how uncompetitive your pay (all external forces!) , your career satisfaction is an inside job.

Motivators Are Enduring

Let's return for a moment to Maslow's Hierarchy of Needs. As we observed earlier, employers tend to focus their attention and budgets on incentives that meet our lower levels of need, what Maslow labeled safety and physiological needs. Our higher-level needs such as belonging are often only addressed by pecking-order improvements in the form of promotions and job titles. In this model, our relationship with work remains largely transactional.

On the other hand, Herzberg identified motivators that take us not only fully into the love/belonging stage with recognition motivators, but into the esteem and self-actualization levels with responsibility, challenging work, and personal growth. By correlation, focusing on what really motivates us in our careers can actually scratch our existential itches at the highest levels! Further–as you might suspect—intrinsic motivation lasts longer than external stimuli do.

In case you're yearning for another psychologist to be included in this discussion, I'll finish with Eric Erickson, an educational psychologist whose last stage of psychosocial development is particularly relevant here. He proposed that as we progress through life we have different stages that present binary questions we must answer. For example, the first is whether or not we will trust the world around us. We take each stage with us through life, culminating in our sixties with Integrity vs. Despair. When we near the last chapter of our lives—coincidentally around traditional retirement age—we are faced with two potential responses to the lives we've lived:

1. My life is coming together into a satisfactory whole. (Integrity)

2. Crap. I blew it. (Despair)

We cannot deny work's impact on our daily lives. But only in the last stage of life do we realize the impact our daily lives had on the tapestry of our existence.

While I'll argue all day long about the merits of career satisfaction, the truth remains that you need both; it's important to have a job that meets your external needs as well as your internal. You can't jump from one ditch to another.

But how do you find that balance? Is it even possible?

In the next chapter, you'll discover not only the right balance for career satisfaction, you'll discover *your* specific combination of internal and external factors that will unlock increased job satisfaction in your current role.

CHAPTER 4

Cracking the Safe:
Discovering your career combination

"Life is like a combination lock;
your job is to find the right
numbers, in the right order, so
you can have everything you
want."
— Brian Tracy

—

thecareerfactors.com

"Hey, Marcus! You look well rested. How was vacation?" greeted Randal the following Monday morning.

"It was great, man. Thanks for asking."

They walked down the long hall in silence before Marcus broached the topic with his colleague. "Remember how lousy I felt about work before I left for vacation?"

"I do. How's that going?"

"Better... I think. I started thinking about the people I know who love their jobs, and I'm starting to understand that work for me is more than just what I do and how much I get paid. That it takes more for me to be happy at work. Does that sound weird?"

"No way, man. I totally get it. What checks those boxes for you?"

"Well, for one, it's the ability to make an impact. I really want my job to matter to someone. Or, I guess, I want the work that I do to last longer than I do. Or something like that. I'm still trying to figure it out."

"Sure! I get that. Remember when I told you that I started thinking differently about my job and that changed things for me?

"I do. What did you mean?"

"When I started here, I had all eyes on the prize: team leader within three years. No one was going to beat me to that spot when Jamie retired. But after two years of grinding and being *mis-er-a-ble*, I realized that I didn't study this in college for the status. I did it because I knew I'd miss being on a team after playing sports for so many years. The most fun I ever had was with a particular group of guys I played ball with growing up. Even one or two years when we weren't that good, we loved playing together. I knew going it alone was going to be no fun, even when I started my career.

I used to think that people who enjoy their jobs had won the lottery, like they pulled the slot machine one time, and—Bingo!—they were in the perfect job. But one day my cousin who works in Atlantic City told me that the same mechanism that produces those beautiful 7s on a slot machine is used to create locks for safes. That's when I started to figure out the one thing that people who love their job have that I didn't. It wasn't luck; it was the right combination.

So far we've talked about how important work is, the variety of influences that likely affected your initial and subsequent career decisions, and how adding intrinsic motivators can increase your job satisfaction.

But those things are still very generalized. Sure, they're backed by research, but how do they apply to you in your current job?

Before we discover the specific combination that will unlock your career satisfaction, it's important to understand a final piece of the puzzle, one that very few people recognize when they begin a career or make decisions about job changes, promotions, or even retirement:

What are you hiring your career to do?

On its face, it's a strange question. Aren't I the one who's getting hired? What does hiring a career even mean?

In behavioral economics there exists a theory that helps explain why people buy what they buy. Commonly known as the "Jobs-to-Be-Done Theory", it proposes that every purchase is made to do a job for the buyer. The cup of coffee I'm enjoying as I write was hired to give me a boost of energy. The shirt you're wearing does the functional job of covering your body according to social norms, but perhaps you also hired it to look great with a pair of pants. You've even hired this book, presumably to help you figure out why some people seem to love their job while you've never felt like you found yourself in the world of work.

I'd like to offer another application of the Jobs-to-Be-Done Theory, one that might help explain the discontent you feel but can't really name. Here it is in two parts:

1. You hired your career to do something for you, to meet a need that's been there for years. Which is only problematic if…

2. You don't know what you hired it to do.

If you apply the Jobs-to-Be-Done theory to your career, you pull back the curtain on your relationship with work. Think of it as a marriage:

Shelly and Aaron date for two years, and Shelly is thrilled when Aaron proposes. They've always talked about a life of adventure and start right away with a honeymoon in Costa Rica, backpacking and ziplining in the rainforest. Even though they must return to "reality" and their respective day jobs, they keep the sense of adventure going on weekend excursions to local destinations and weeklong voyages to other countries twice a year.

But after a few years, Shelly starts looking for another adventure: starting a family. It's never been on her radar before, but now she can't help but see babies wherever she goes and has the strongest urge to be a mother. She makes up her mind to tell Aaron at dinner that night.

Before she can get the words out, Aaron blurts out his own good news: he has been offered a job from a former boss that includes a sizeable increase in pay and regular travel to corporate locations all over the world. He is ecstatic because Shelly can work remotely and they can finally live the way they want to all the time instead of just fitting in mini-adventures here and there.

Shelly is happy for him but believes that her desire to start a family will have to wait. She can't stand in the

39

way of this opportunity for Aaron. Besides, she really loves travel, and it would be fun to see parts of the world they haven't yet.

Six months into this next chapter of their life together, Shelly realizes that her desire to be a mother won't wait, especially when she visits her sister after her niece was born. She begins to resent the frequent getaways that work within Aaron's new schedule, and the excitement that travel used to bring is replaced with boredom. Aaron no longer has an enthusiastic wife to share his work wins with, so he stops sharing them and begins to spend more time at work, reducing the weekly excursions to monthly... and sometimes alone.

What they once had in common has become a point of contention: Shelly resenting Aaron's job for delaying the start of their family, and Aaron confused by Shelly's seemingly overnight change in behavior. And neither knows what to do about it.

And that's the same thing that happens with your career: You either don't know what you really want from it or you don't know how to communicate when that priority changes.

That's where the Career Factors come in.

The Career Factors is a process for identifying what you want from your job and then creating a lens for seeing and experiencing it in your current job; done right, it can even be a decision matrix for future opportunities.

If—as we discussed earlier—you're more likely to treasure what you can measure, I propose a solution: let's start measuring what we want to treasure. Enter the Career Factors.

The Career Factors are made of six distinct job satisfaction—and dissatisfaction—contributors, some of which you've seen in our discussion so far. You'll notice that while each is important on its own, some will jump out to you as more important than others. How they work together to enhance each other is also vital to understanding your unique Career Factors.

Skills: You want a career where you can use your strengths, skills, and talents on a regular basis. When you do this, you leave end work each day being more filled up than used up. You feel competent in your career, which gives you the confidence to take on new challenges in your current role.

Impact: You want a career that makes a difference in other people's lives. When you're in a role that makes an impact, you're able to overcome obstacles and bad days because you're focused on the mission. You love rallying others to your projects because you know that what you're doing matters.

Relationships: No matter what the job is, the people you work with either make or break your experience. You might not love your current role, but your career satisfaction is largely based on your relationships with those you collaborate with on a regular basis. They're the ones who keep you going when the going gets tough.

Environment: People like you really value their physical surroundings and try to create ideal working conditions so they can do their best work. You likely recognize that your working environment affects you in a variety of ways, so you prioritize it when making decisions about which roles to pursue with which companies.

Growth: In your case, the best roles are the ones that provide opportunities to gain skills, improve communication, develop new ways of thinking, and become better on your way to career advancement. You recognize the value of both "hard" and "soft" skills as a means to improving your life as your career develops.

Lifestyle: While your career is important, you're keenly aware of how much it can affect your life, so you prioritize the time you spend outside of work, whether with family and friends, traveling and pursuing hobbies, or serving non-profits. You're grateful for what your career provides you, but you aren't a workaholic. Your deathbed regret won't be, "I wish I would have spent more time at the office."

Now that you have a general idea of what each is, I invite you to take the free diagnostic at thecareerfactors.com to discover your top three Career Factors, the combination to unlocking career satisfaction in your current job. Once you've taken it, record the date and your score. I've included multiple spaces for your results because your Career Factors combination can change over time, and it's good to track it over seasons of life.

Date: _____
CF3: _____, _____, _____

Date: _____
CF3: _____, _____, _____

Date: _____
CF3: _____, _____, _____

Date: _____
CF3: _____, _____, _____

Date: _____
CF3: _____, _____, _____

Sam Feeney's Career Factors

CHAPTER 5

Owning Your Career Factors:
Creating Your Unique Combination for Job
Satisfaction

Define success on your own
terms, achieve it by your own
rules, and build a life you're
proud to live.
— Anne Sweeney

―

thecareerfactors.com

For the next week, Marcus reflected on his conversation with Randal. The list he had made on vacation was beginning to look like the key ingredients to create someone's perfect job: Skills, Impact, Relationships, Environment, Growth, and Lifestyle. Everything that he could think of that made someone happy—or unhappy—in their career could fit into one of those main categories. What was crazy, too, was that he and Randal had the same job, but they enjoyed it for different reasons, so the job description wasn't the thing that made him happy; it was what he wanted from it… and whether it was able to deliver.

Now that he knew more about what motivated people at work, Marcus had seen what he was calling Career Factors everywhere, particularly his top three of Impact, Growth, and Lifestyle. His antennae were always up for examples of the code he seemed to have cracked, not only in himself but in others he worked with.

But something was missing, and he couldn't put his finger on it until Jacqui brought up the subject of work over dinner Friday night.

"You seem to have been in a good mood this week. Is work going well?"

"It's going great, actually. I've been thinking about a new way to understand what makes people tick at work, and it's really interesting. I might be on to something here."

Marcus explained what he was learning about the Career Factors, including the idea that each person has a certain combination and that people can have the same job but different motivators...or the same motivators but different jobs.

When he paused for a bite of his meal, Jacqui inserted a question. "I really like this, babe. And I like that you like it. I haven't seen you excited about something work-related in a while."

"This idea makes a lot of sense to me, and I can see how it applies to people in my job. My counterpart, Marcie, for example, is very particular about her workspace. If she can work uninterrupted from 1:00 to 3:00 every afternoon, she's totally fine with unscheduled drop-ins at other times. But if you enter "the sanctuary" during those hours, you are in for it.

"And Stephen is quickly disinterested in projects that aren't what he calls 'the highest and best use of his talents.' I used to think that was him trying to get out of work, but when he does get a chance to use his skills, there are few better in the industry, let alone our company."

"Exactly!" Marcus agreed. "And Monique from payroll. She could get a better job tomorrow with all of her experience, but she loves the people she works with, so she wouldn't think of leaving."

"Do you mean she could get a better job, or one that pays more?" Jacqui smiled.

Marcus chuckled. "You got me. I'm still thinking that what you get paid is the only measurement of whether a job is good or not."

"I have a question, though, about this theory—or whatever we're calling it," Jacqui offered. "What are you specifically looking for in your three areas? I know you said one of them is Impact, and I think that fits you perfectly. But that means different things to different people. My job helps my co-workers do their jobs better by making sure the tech systems are running smoothly. But what would that look like for you?"

As Marcus thought about all the ways people can make an impact through their work, he saw that only **he** could provide clear definitions for his Career Factors. But that when he did—when he took the time to clarify what he wanted from his career—he would have the power to not only make better decisions about his career, but to apply those Career Factors to his current job.

Now that you know what your top three Career Factors are, it's important to identify exactly what they look like to **you**. While you may share some of these factors with others you know and work with, your career motivators mean something unique to you and therefore might be very different from those around you, affecting your respective career satisfaction in very different ways.

Let's say that you and I each have Impact as our number 1 Career Factor. (Impact is almost always in my top 2, in case you're wondering.) On the surface, it would appear that we have a lot in common given we have the same career motivator. However, when we each explore our unique meaning of Impact, we might discover that we're more different than alike.

I'm reminded of a co-worker, Trish. Both of us were school counselors in a large, suburban high school who were motivated by the desire to make an impact. But our definitions of Impact were very different. She had a heart for the kids who had a lot of issues, those whose trauma in life had hampered their ability to thrive in a normal school setting or who lacked the coping skills to deal with much of the relational drama that high school can present. Trish's office reflected her approach to impacting kids: she had a rocking chair and pillow in the corner for whomever needed it.

On the other hand, my desire to make an impact in my career showed up in very different ways. Trish wanted to help a small group of students make dramatic changes in their lives. In effect, her picture of Impact was a mile deep and an inch wide; by contrast, Impact for me was systemic, a yearning to help many people—students and teachers alike—by improving the way we did things as a district. I often worked on initiatives that would give our students more access to interesting programs and opportunities, challenging the status quo when colleagues and administrators balked at my suggestions for improvement.

As a result, Trish and I often butted heads, **even though we were both motivated by Impact!** As you will with others in your life if you assume commonalities that only exist on the surface or in labels.

The remainder of this chapter details several ways that each of the Career Factors might show up for you. They are simply ideas to get you thinking about what it looks like to enjoy a particular career motivator so you can create a vision for the perfect career using your Career Factors.

Many have also found it helpful to reflect on jobs they've had in the past to identify keys to a fulfilling work experience; even a job that you left likely had one or two features that you enjoyed. Or you may find clues to your ideal career in whatever has caused discontent in previous or current roles. We don't always know what we want, but we very often can identify what we don't want, so this exercise can reveal our career motivators in inverse.

However you come approach it, at the end of the chapter are three pages designed to help you capture the picture of each of your top three Career Factors so you have an ideal that you can use as a lens for your current job, which we'll get to in chapter 7.

Skills

What does your desire to use your skills at work look like in an ideal situation?

Autonomy: Autonomy at work means having the freedom and independence to make decisions and take actions related to your job without constant supervision or direction from others. It means having control over how you perform your work and being trusted to make decisions that align with the goals and objectives of your organization.

Some examples of autonomy in the workplace might include

- Setting your own work schedule or determining how you allocate your time
- Making decisions related to how you approach a particular project or task
- Having the ability to choose the tools or methods you use to complete your work
- Being empowered to make decisions related to your area of expertise or responsibility
- Having the ability to take initiative and suggest new ideas or approaches to your work

Strengths into Superpowers: Turning your skills at work into superpowers means leveraging your unique abilities and talents to become a standout performer in your field. It involves developing and refining your skills to the point where you can use them to achieve exceptional results and make a significant impact in your organization.

Staying in your lane: Staying in your lane at work means focusing on your specific area of expertise or responsibility and not getting involved in areas outside of your scope of work. It means working within the boundaries of your role and not overstepping into other areas that may be better left to other colleagues or departments.

Compensating for weaknesses: No one is perfect, and everyone has areas where they are less skilled or knowledgeable. By working in a team, you can complement your strengths with the strengths of others. For example, if you are great at coming up with creative ideas but struggle with details, you might work with someone who is more detail-oriented to ensure that all aspects of the project are covered.

Impact

What does your desire to make an impact at work look like in an ideal situation?

Scale: To impact others at scale means to have a significant and far-reaching effect on a large number of people or communities. It involves creating a broad and systemic change that can benefit many individuals or groups, rather than focusing on individual or localized impacts.

Impacting others at scale requires a deliberate and strategic approach that considers the broader social and economic systems that affect people's lives. It often involves leveraging technology, media, or other tools to reach a larger audience and amplify the impact of your efforts.

Examples of impact at scale include initiatives that address widespread social issues, such as poverty, inequality, or environmental degradation. It can involve creating educational programs, developing new technologies, advocating for policy changes, or implementing large-scale community development projects.

Depth: To impact others deeply means to have a significant and meaningful effect on someone's life or experience. It goes beyond surface-level interactions or shallow connections and instead involves creating a lasting impression or change in someone's life.

When you impact others deeply, you make a difference in their lives in a way that they will remember and appreciate for a long time. This might involve providing emotional support during a difficult time, offering guidance or mentorship, inspiring someone to pursue their dreams, or helping someone to overcome a challenge or obstacle.

Deeply impacting others can also involve being a positive role model or influence, setting an example of kindness, empathy, or excellence that others can learn from and aspire to. It can involve using your skills and talents to make a difference in the world, whether through your work, volunteerism, or other activities.

Audience: To make a difference to a specific group of people means to have a positive and meaningful impact on a particular community, demographic, or group of individuals. It involves identifying the unique needs and challenges faced by that group and taking action to address them in a way that creates positive change and improves their quality of life.

Making a difference to a specific group of people can involve a wide range of activities and initiatives, depending on the nature of the group and the issues they face. Examples might include:

- Developing programs or services that meet the specific needs of a particular community or demographic, such as seniors, people with disabilities, or low-income families.
- Advocating for policy changes that address the unique challenges faced by a particular group, such as improving access to healthcare or education.
- Providing mentorship or support to individuals within a specific group, such as youth or new immigrants, to help them achieve their goals and overcome barriers.
- Raising awareness and promoting understanding of the issues faced by a particular group, to help reduce stigma or discrimination and create a more inclusive society.

This requires a deep understanding of the needs and challenges faced by that group, as well as a commitment to taking action and creating positive change. It can involve working collaboratively with community members, organizations, and other stakeholders to achieve common goals, and may require creativity, innovation, and persistence to overcome obstacles and make a lasting impact.

Aligning personal mission: Aligning your personal mission with your company's mission can help you to feel more engaged and motivated in your work and can also contribute to the overall success of your organization. Here are some steps you can take to align your personal mission with your company's mission:

- Understand your personal mission: Take some time to reflect on your own values, goals, and priorities. Consider what drives you and what you hope to achieve in your career and life.
- Understand your company's mission: Review your organization's mission statement and values and consider how they align with your own personal mission. Look for areas of overlap or alignment.
- Identify areas of common ground: Identify specific areas where your personal mission and your company's mission align. For example, if your personal mission is to make a positive impact on the environment, and your company is committed to sustainability, there may be opportunities to align your work with those goals.
- Communicate with your manager or colleagues: Discuss your personal mission with your manager or colleagues and explore opportunities to align your work with the company's mission. They may be able to provide guidance or support in identifying projects or initiatives that align with your values and goals.
- Take action: Once you have identified areas of alignment, take action to incorporate those values and goals into your work. Look for opportunities to make a positive impact within your organization and be proactive in seeking out ways to contribute to the company's mission.

Relationships

What does your desire to have meaningful relationships at work look like in an ideal situation?

Collaboration: Collaboration at work is a process where two or more people work together to achieve a common goal or outcome. It involves sharing knowledge, skills, and resources to accomplish tasks or projects, and requires effective communication, mutual respect, and a willingness to work together towards a shared objective.
Collaboration at work can take many different forms, depending on the nature of the project or task at hand.

Some examples might include

- Teamwork on a project: Collaborating with colleagues on a shared project or task, where each team member brings their unique skills and expertise to the table.
- Cross-functional collaboration: Working with individuals from different departments or areas of expertise to achieve a common goal, such as developing a new product or service.
- Collaborative problem-solving: Working together to identify and solve complex problems or challenges, drawing on each other's strengths and expertise.
- Collaborative learning: Sharing knowledge and skills with others and learning from their experiences and perspectives.

Belonging: Workplace relationships can create a sense of belonging by providing employees with a sense of connection, support, and community within the workplace. When employees feel that they are part of a larger team or community, they are more likely to feel invested in their work and to be motivated to do their best.

Here are some ways that workplace relationships can create a sense of belonging:

Social connections: When employees feel that they have positive relationships with their colleagues and managers, they are more likely to feel a sense of connection and belonging within the workplace. Regular social interactions, such as team lunches or after-work drinks, can help to foster these connections.

Support and encouragement: When employees feel that they have the support of their colleagues and managers, they are more likely to feel confident in their abilities and motivated to succeed. Encouragement and support from colleagues can help to build trust and create a sense of community within the workplace.

Shared goals and values: When employees feel that they are working towards a common goal or purpose, they are more likely to feel a sense of belonging within the workplace. This can be reinforced through regular communication about the organization's values and mission, and by recognizing and celebrating achievements as a team.

Recognition and appreciation: When employees feel that their contributions are valued and appreciated by their colleagues and managers, they are more likely to feel a sense of belonging and commitment to the organization. Regular recognition and appreciation can help to reinforce positive relationships and foster a sense of community within the workplace.

Diverse perspectives: When working in a team, you are likely to encounter people with different backgrounds, experiences, and perspectives. This can help to broaden your own perspective and complement your strengths with fresh ideas and approaches.

Skill sharing: Working in a team allows you to share your own skills and knowledge with others, while also learning from their expertise. This can help to develop new skills and improve existing ones and can complement your strengths by providing you with a wider range of capabilities.

Increased efficiency: By working in a team, you can divide tasks and responsibilities in a way that complements each team member's strengths. This can help to improve efficiency and productivity, as each person can focus on the tasks that they are best suited for.

Environment

What does your desire to have a positive work environment look like in an ideal situation?

Pace: The pace of a work environment refers to the speed and intensity at which work is done and tasks are completed. The pace of a work environment can vary depending on several factors, including the nature of the work, the industry, the size of the organization, and the culture of the workplace.

Culture: Workplace culture refers to the shared values, beliefs, attitudes, behaviors, and practices that shape the working environment of an organization. It encompasses everything from the way people communicate and interact with each other to the organization's mission, vision, and overall business strategy.

A strong workplace culture is characterized by a shared sense of purpose, mutual respect, and a positive work environment. It is one where employees feel valued, supported, and encouraged to bring their best selves to work each day. Some of the key elements of a positive workplace culture might be

- Clear communication: Effective communication is essential for building trust and fostering a positive work environment. This means that employees should feel comfortable sharing their ideas, feedback, and concerns, and that managers should be open and transparent in their communication with employees.
- Collaborative teamwork: Collaboration is key to creating a sense of unity and shared purpose within an organization. Teams should be encouraged to work together, share their skills and expertise, and support each other in achieving their goals.

- A focus on employee well-being: Workplace culture should prioritize employee well-being, both in terms of physical health and mental well-being. This might include providing access to wellness programs, mental health resources, and opportunities for work-life balance.
- Respect and inclusion: A positive workplace culture values diversity and promotes a sense of inclusion for all employees. This means creating an environment where everyone feels valued, respected, and supported, regardless of their background or identity.

Schedule: There are several varieties of work schedules that exist in the modern workplace. Some common examples are

- Full-time: A full-time work schedule typically consists of 40 hours per week, usually spread out over five days. This is the standard schedule for many jobs in industries such as retail, hospitality, and healthcare.
- Part-time: Part-time schedules involve working fewer hours than full-time schedules. Part-time schedules may be ideal for students or individuals who need to balance work with other commitments.
- Flex-time: Flex-time schedules allow employees to work outside of traditional business hours. For example, an employee might work four 10-hour days per week instead of five 8-hour days. This type of schedule can provide greater work-life balance

for employees with family or other personal obligations.

- Job sharing: Job sharing involves two or more employees sharing the responsibilities of a single full-time job. This can be a good option for employees who want to work part-time but still maintain the benefits of a full-time position.

- Shift work: Shift work involves working non-traditional hours, such as overnight or on weekends. This type of schedule is common in industries such as manufacturing, transportation, and emergency services.

- Remote work: Remote work schedules allow employees to work from home or other off-site locations. This type of schedule can be beneficial for employees who have long commutes or prefer a more flexible work environment.

- Compressed work week: A compressed work week involves working a full-time schedule in fewer than five days. For example, an employee might work four 10-hour days per week instead of five 8-hour days.

Work setting and environment can refer to both the physical setting in which you work and the overall culture and atmosphere of your workplace. Some factors that are part of the work setting and environment are

- Physical layout: The physical layout of your workplace, including the design and layout of your workspace and the overall layout of the building or office.

- Comfort and ergonomics: The comfort and ergonomics of your workspace, including factors such as lighting, ventilation, temperature, and the design of your desk and chair.
- Amenities: The amenities that are available in your workplace, such as break rooms, outdoor areas, and any other resources or facilities that are available for employees to use.
- Company culture: The overall culture and atmosphere of your workplace, including the values and expectations of the organization, the level of support and collaboration among employees, and the overall tone and feel of the workplace.
- Workload and demands: The workload and demands of your job, including the amount of work you are expected to complete and the level of stress and pressure you experience on the job.

Growth

What does your desire to grow personally and/or professionally at work look like in an ideal situation?

Your job can help you become a better person in a number of ways. Some ways that your job can help you grow personally include:

- Personal growth opportunities: Many jobs offer opportunities for personal growth, such as professional development programs, mentorship programs, and leadership development programs, which can help you acquire new skills and knowledge and grow as a person.

- Sense of accomplishment: Achieving goals and making a positive impact in your job can give you a sense of accomplishment and pride, which can help you feel more confident and motivated to continue growing as a person.
- Personal values alignment: If your job aligns with your personal values and beliefs, it can give you a sense of purpose and meaning in your work, which can help you feel more fulfilled and motivated to be your best self.
- Personal growth opportunities: Many jobs offer opportunities for personal growth, such as professional development programs, mentorship programs, and leadership development programs, which can help you acquire new skills and knowledge and grow as a person.

Your career might also include the following professional growth potential:

- Professional development training: Many organizations offer professional development training or courses to help employees grow and develop new skills. This can include in-house training programs, online courses, or workshops and conferences.
- Mentorship: Many organizations have mentorship programs that match employees with more experienced colleagues who can provide guidance and support as they develop their skills and careers.
- Leadership development: Some organizations offer leadership development programs or opportunities for employees to take on leadership roles within the organization, which can provide

valuable experience and help employees grow and develop their leadership skills.

- Job rotation: Some organizations offer job rotation programs that allow employees to take on temporary assignments in different departments or teams, which can provide a chance to learn new skills and gain a broader understanding of the organization.
- Educational opportunities: Some organizations offer tuition reimbursement or other educational opportunities that can help employees further their education and expand their skills and knowledge.
- Promotion or advancement opportunities: Many organizations have promotion or advancement opportunities that can allow you to take on more responsibility and move up within the organization.

Lifestyle

What does your desire to create a fulfilling look like in an ideal situation?

Lifestyle refers to the way in which you live your life. It includes your daily routines, habits, and activities, as well as the choices you make about how you spend your time and resources. Lifestyle also includes the values, beliefs, and goals that shape your decisions and actions. Your lifestyle can have a significant impact on your overall well-being and quality of life, and it is often influenced by factors such as your work, family, social connections, and personal interests and hobbies.

Work can have a significant impact on your lifestyle in a number of ways. Some ways that work can affect your lifestyle include

- Financial stability: Work can provide you with a steady income, which can help you to meet your financial needs and provide financial stability for you and your family.
- Work-life balance: Your job can impact your work-life balance, which is the balance between your professional and personal responsibilities and commitments. A job that allows you to achieve a good work-life balance can help you to be more productive and fulfilled in your work, which can in turn improve your overall quality of life.
- Health insurance and other benefits: Many jobs offer health insurance and other benefits such as retirement plans, which can help you to manage your health and financial needs.
- Social connections: Your job can provide you with the opportunity to form social connections with your coworkers, which can provide support, encouragement, and a sense of community.

Your job can affect your lifestyle in a number of ways, including

- Income: Your job is likely your primary source of income, which can have a major impact on your lifestyle. The amount you earn can determine where you live, what type of car you drive, the quality of food you eat, and more.
- Time: The amount of time you spend working can also impact your lifestyle. If you work long hours,

you may have less time for hobbies, socializing, or other activities that contribute to a balanced lifestyle.

- Stress: Some jobs can be more stressful than others, and this stress can spill over into other areas of your life. High-stress jobs can lead to burnout, poor sleep, and a reduced quality of life.

Hopefully you've gotten a sense of how much more complex each of the Career Factors can be and started to clarify what your top three career motivators might look like in an ideal work situation. Take a few minutes and start sketching out your unique take on the Career Factors on the following pages so you can identify what really matters to you at work.

My #1 Career Factor: _____

What it looks like in an ideal working world: _____

_____

_____

_____

_____

_____

_____

_____

_____

_____

_____

_____

_____

_____

My #2 Career Factor: _____

What it looks like in an ideal working world: _____

_____

_____

_____

_____

_____

_____

_____

_____

_____

_____

_____

_____

_____

My #3 Career Factor: _____

What it looks like in an ideal working world: _____

_____

_____

_____

_____

_____

_____

_____

_____

_____

_____

_____

_____

_____

CHAPTER 6

An Inside Job:
Why career satisfaction is your responsibility… and why that's a good thing

"In the long run, we shape our lives, and we shape ourselves. The process never ends until we die. And the choices we make are ultimately our own responsibility."
— Eleanor Roosevelt

thecareerfactors.com

For the next three weeks, Marcus tried to open the lock to his career satisfaction at work, only to become more and more frustrated. He knew that his top three motivators were Impact, Growth, and Lifestyle, but the more he focused on them, the more he noticed what was lacking. He slowly and regrettably became convinced that he would be forced to change jobs in order to find it. This job could never make him happy because it couldn't give him what he was looking for. He scheduled an appointment with Fran in human resources for the following Tuesday and reached out a friend of his who was always trying to get him to work with him.

The next Tuesday, Marcus met with Fran to discuss his situation. He remembered her from the hiring process, but they hadn't interacted much since then, so he really wasn't sure what to expect.

To his surprise, Fran seemed saddened by the news that he was considering leaving.

"I'm so sorry to hear that, Marcus. I've heard only great things about you during your time here. Is there anything we can do to keep you?"

Marcus shook his head. "Not unless you have a magic wand. You see, I finally figured out the perfect job for me: one that makes an impact, that allows me to grow personally, and that provides me a family-first lifestyle.

"But it's almost like now that I know the combination for my career, I need to find the job that the combination will unlock, if that makes sense. So I think I need to leave."

Fran sat back in her chair and thought for a moment, her eyes never leaving him. "May I speak frankly, Marcus?" she asked.

"Fire away," Marcus allowed.

"I'm so pleased that you've discovered this combination or recipe. It's incredibly rare to know what you're looking for in... well, in any part of life. So, congratulations to you on this. I mean it.

"But do you know what's even more rare?"

Marcus shook his head, but remained silent, waiting for her to answer.

"What's more rare than knowing what you're looking for is *finding it*. I've been here a long time, as you may know, and I have hired hundreds of people over the years. And I've helped many of them move on to what I hope are better opportunities. Some grow where they're planted, and others hop from job to job, looking for the place where everything will be perfect.

"What I've learned is that whether it's here or at another company or even in their own businesses, the ones who create thriving careers are the ones who are willing to do the work to find what they're looking for."

Marcus was surprised. *Do the work? What does that mean?* His skepticism must have been written on his face because Fran addressed it.

"Think about it this way: most people have an unrealistic view of their employer. On the one hand, their boss can do nothing right. It's like a corollary of Murphy's Law: Everything that can go wrong... is the boss's fault. On the other hand, employees place all of the responsibility for their job satisfaction in their company's hands. It's a no-win situation, one that I have to hear about more times than you can imagine.

"Yes, we could be doing more to make an impact as a company, to provide opportunities for you to grow as a person and as a professional, and..."

"And to have a lifestyle that prioritizes my family," Marcus finished.

"Yes, and to give you the balance you need to be a great dad and a great employee. We could do more in those areas." She paused.

"But so could you, Marcus."

I'm going to warn you right now: you might have the most trouble with this chapter. Not understanding it; accepting it. But if you've been with me this far, tracking with my premise that there's a new way to do career satisfaction, then stick with me just a little longer. This part is crucial.

Here it is: **career satisfaction is an inside job**. More to the point, **you** are responsible—at least in part—for how you feel about your job.

Don't get me wrong. There are many things your supervisor or company could be doing differently, but at the end of the day, your happiness at work depends largely on you.

Would you have it any other way?

Given the amount of our lives we spend at work and the impact those hours, weeks, and years have on all the other parts of our lives, our work is an undeniable part of our legacy, the tapestry we're weaving every day. Do you really want to leave it up to someone else?

As we discussed in previous chapters, understanding career satisfaction as more elegant than just what you do and how much you get paid allows us to consider some internal motivators like whether your job makes an impact or the quality of your relationships at work. That's a huge step to increasing your career satisfaction.

But even if we clearly identify the key characteristics in each of our top three Career Factors, a fulfilling and rewarding career will remain out of reach if we rely on others to make things happen. Like the would-be triathlete, if I'm wearing workout clothes and watching videos by fitness influencers but stay on the couch, I'm only going to be frustrated with my lack of progress.

Career satisfaction has long been seen as an outside-in phenomenon that really included just two factors—competency and compensation—with the general consensus being that the employer determines both. Even extending the ingredients of career satisfaction to include working conditions and collegial relationships, a trend emerges: these are all external factors, dependent on others to be either good or bad. And that's bad for employees for two reasons.

First, it creates an unhealthy imbalance in our relationship with our employers. If we wait around for our employers to create the perfect conditions for our career fulfillment, we are not only setting ourselves up for disappointment, we are also setting them up for failure. How can they be expected to focus on what makes each of us happy in our work with all the other balls they have to juggle?

And it's not that they don't care, despite what movies like *Horrible Bosses*, *Office Space*, and *Joe Versus the Volcano* purport. They just have a lot going on, especially above them on the organizational chart. Heck, would you want your supervisor's job? Especially considering the way people talk about him or her behind their back?

Think of the demands a supervisor faces in keeping every employee happy. It's akin to a short order cook who works in a restaurant with no menu. Each customer wants a different meal, but they don't know what the options are, so they take forever to decide.

Only the really demanding or needy customers get the cook's attention, and they're never happy with what they end up getting. And the cook starts snapping at everyone, which creates animosity between the restaurant and all of the customers.

Second, employers are not equipped to accurately determine your and my job satisfaction. Unfortunately, the best tools that managers use to measure employee engagement often perpetuate an outside-in approach to career satisfaction, including powerhouses like Gallup's Q12 survey. As McKinsey Affiliate Advisor Aaron McHugh notes in his book *Fire Your Boss*,

> "Gallup's targeted inquiries drill into key questions like:
> - "Does the mission / purpose of your company make you feel your job is important?"
> - In the last seven days, have you received recognition or praise for doing good work?"
> - In the last year, have you had opportunities to learn and grow?"

Good questions? On the surface, no doubt. We all want to be part of a mission we believe in, be applauded for doing great work, and develop personally and professionally. But there's a fatal flaw within Gallup's underlying assumption. We, *you and I,* are absolved from any personal responsibility, and 100 percent of the solution rests in the hands of our employers.

And this is where I'm calling BS. We need to take and remain in charge of stewarding our own happiness" (22-23).

And so I assert that career satisfaction is an inside job, the product of empowered individuals with an internal locus of control, who take responsibility for their engagement and partner with management to find solutions.

If you're starting to warm up to the assertion that career satisfaction is an inside job, great. Thanks for sticking with me. If you're still resistant—and that's totally understandable given that I'm upending a decades-long perception that we inherited from our parents—then allow me to discuss my favorite part of an inside-out career satisfaction model: the benefits.

Internal locus of control

The term *locus of control* describes the tendency of an individual to explain the outcomes in their lives. Someone with an external locus of control often blames other people and circumstances for the way things turn out, while someone who possesses an internal locus of control recognizes the role they played in how a project went... or didn't.

According to HRDQ, a resource for personal development for the past forty years, an internal locus of control improves your workplace performance in the following ways:

- It makes you more likely to love your career
- Employees with a high internal locus of control are more likely to give their all at work
- It means you handle stress better
- It makes you more goal-oriented

- It empowers you to take responsibility for your circumstances

A word that can be used interchangeably with internal locus of control is **agency**, and it probably best encapsulates the benefits of internal locus of control. When you and I have agency, we have power in a situation, no matter how dire. I think of it as a toolbox that I can pull out and use time and time again, and the more I use the tools, the more confident I am in being able to address whatever challenge or obstacle I face.

Improvement

When you have agency, you have the opportunity to focus only on the things you can control, which will eventually result in improvement in those areas. As an exercise, take a moment to complete the chart below about a particular challenge you're facing at work.

The challenge: _____

Things that matter at work but that I cannot control:
1.
2.
3.
4.
5.
6.
7.
8.
9.
10.

Things I can influence at work:
1.
2.
3.
4.
5.
6.
7.
8.
9.
10.

This exercise, presented as the Circle of Influence and the Circle of Concern in Stephen Covey's *7 Habits of Highly Effective People*, empowers us to recognize that there are a number of things that might be bothering us about what's going on at work or in politics or with our children, but that only by focusing on the first column can we do anything to change it. It's a simultaneously empowering and sobering realization!

Covey asserted that we can only focus on one column or the other—never both at the same time—and whichever column we focus on grows. As a result, we increase either our influence or our feeling of powerlessness. Which would you prefer? When we focus on what we can influence, we grow in those areas, improving our competence and confidence and bringing more opportunities our way.

Putting this into practice, let's examine the six Career Factors through the lens of internally derived career satisfaction. How might you and I be responsible for our sense of fulfillment in each? I'll provide examples from my work experience and offer you the chance to fine tune your top three in the next chapter.

Skills: Being able to use my talents and abilities on a regular basis

Inside-out job satisfaction: While I can't change my job description, I can choose specific areas of focus on projects that align with what I'm good at. The continued focus allows me to become the in-house expert on certain topics and a resource to my colleagues, which leads to them volunteering me for similar (preferred) tasks in the future.

Impact: Work that improves the lives of others in some way

Inside-out job satisfaction: Initially I was excited to work with the clientele my position served, but that faded with time. However, I realized I can make an impact on others at work—in this case, my colleagues—by creating trainings that allow them to spend more time making the impact that motivated them.

Relationships: The positive transactional and transformational interactions with others at work

Inside-out job satisfaction: There were a few people in my department whose mindset and decisions exasperated me on a regular basis. Instead of continually focusing on how annoying they were, I began to be intentional about who I was spending time with outside of structured meetings, deliberately surrounding myself with positive people.

Environment: The workplace setting and culture that affects our performance

Inside-out job satisfaction: Much of my working environment was chaotic and unpredictable, but I could control my workspace and my calendar in a few important ways. I chose how I decorated my office, which set the tone for many of my meetings. I also blocked out thirty minutes for lunch in my calendar every day. Even if I just ate lunch at my desk, no one could book me for a meeting without going through me. Small wins are still wins!

Growth: Opportunities to improve personally and professionally

Inside-out job satisfaction: Much of my compulsory professional development felt like hand-me-down clothing: ill-fitting because it was designed for someone else. However, I discovered that HR was open to suggestions and would approve pretty much anything that I presented as an alternative. I got to pursue personal and professional improvement that fit my goals.

Lifestyle: The intersection of time and money

Inside-out job satisfaction: A very early start to the workday was a drag on my evenings—no fun when your wife's a night owl—but the schedule allowed time in the afternoons to hang out with my kids and even coach sports, which I only fully appreciated when speaking to friends who worked traditional 9-5 jobs.

I hope by these examples you see that I could have relied solely on my employer or the circumstances of my job to determine how I felt about my career. Instead, I increased my agency and became something of a subject matter expert in a few areas by focusing on what I could control, which led to increased opportunities at work and beyond. Like writing this book, for example. Let's bring an inside-out approach to career satisfaction with us to our penultimate chapter.

CHAPTER 7

Acres of Diamonds:
Putting your Career Factors to work in
your current role

"Your diamonds are not in far
distant mountains or in
yonder seas; they are in your
own backyard, if you but dig
for them."
– Russell Conwell

---

thecareerfactors.com

Marcus was still smarting from his interaction with Fran as he shared the encounter with Jacqui over dinner that evening.

"What did you say?" his wife asked, surprised at (and a little amused by) the HR director's frankness.

"What could I say? I just sat there for a minute and said, 'Wow. Well, I think I'll go now.' And I got up and left."

"What did she say in response?" Jacqui asked, trying to suppress a smile at the scene her husband described.

"She was very nice. She said that she'd love to help me find my 'acres of diamonds'—or something like that—if I wanted help. Of course, she had to kind of yell that last part because I was already outside her door, so I'm not sure what she meant."

"Well, what do you think about what she said: that *you* could do more in the areas you think will lead to happiness in your job?"

"I guess she's right. My immediate response was to be pretty mad about what she said. I mean, doesn't the company control all the things that make employees happy? Isn't it their responsibility?

Jacqui loved a challenge and thought for a minute before posing a suggestion. "I know what you mean. After all, they make all the decisions; you and I were hired to help them reach respective goals. But if your idea about job satisfaction is true—and I'm beginning to think you're right—then it's up to each of us to find our definition of happiness in our jobs, right?"

Marcus nodded.

"And you've been asking—but never actually asking because you didn't even know what you were asking for!—your boss to help you make an impact and get better and put your family first.

Marcus laughed sheepishly, "Puts them in a pretty tough spot, doesn't it?

"I'm not trying to be mean here, but," Jacqui paused. "Those are a big deal. Legacy stuff. Do you want them to be in sole control of getting those things?"

"You're right. I didn't want it to be that way. And there's no way it could be. How can a few people who run a company know and cater to hundreds of employees' individual career motivations? It's like trying to hit a dartboard in the dark. It's just not possible.

"The more I understand my career factors and what I want from my job, the more I realize that it's—at least in part—up to me to scratch those itches. Even in my current role."

The next day, Marcus ran into Randal in the staff kitchen and shared his conversations with Fran and Jacqui.

"That's a crazy day, bro! So, are you still thinking about quitting?" Randal asked.

"I don't think so, but I'm not really sure what to do next. I agree with Jacqui that it's at least partly up to me to be happy in my job no matter where I'm working. And I want it to be that way because then I control my job satisfaction, not someone else's company policy.

But if I'm not going to wait around for someone to make a change, how can I increase or improve what makes me happy in my job?"

Randal considered this and then asked, "What did you say your motivation combo or code or whatever you call it is?"

"I'm going with factors for the moment," replied Marcus, "and they're making an impact, growing personally, and having a family-first lifestyle."

"And you'd like more of those things here?" Randal clarified.

"Right. Think I can, or should I bail and work somewhere else?"

"Well, you're already making a big impact by helping athletes get back to full strength sooner. Doesn't that make you happy about your job?"

"Yeah, it does. But I think I want something bigger or longer lasting than that. It feels too temporary."

"Okay. Well, how about the company Volunteer Day? That helps a ton of people in bigger ways than taping an ankle."

"I love that day! I just ran into one of the families we helped, and they were so grateful for what we did for them. It seems weird to say, but I think I got more out of it than they did.

"But isn't that day already organized and set up ahead of time by somebody as part of their job?" Marcus challenged.

"I'm sure it is, but have you ever had someone refuse an offer for help? Whoever runs that—I think it's somebody in HR—probably got handed that as part of their job description but is pretty busy with what they actually get paid to do to make it what it could be."

"In fact, I wonder if making an impact is low on what they want from their job!" Randal smiled. "You'd actually be doing them a favor by helping."

"That's great," Marcus agreed, "but should I be working here to make an impact for two days a year? Shouldn't I just go work for a non-profit if I want to make an impact?"

Randal considered his question for a moment before replying. "You said that you want your impact to be bigger or last longer than just helping an athlete get back on the field, right?"

"That's right," Marcus agreed.

"Have you ever had that experience, where someone left better because of their interaction with you?"

Marcus immediately thought of Jayson and relayed the story of a young man who had suffered a season-ending injury and was feeling neglected by his coaches because his replacement was doing so well in his spot. Marcus took time during Jayson's rehabilitation to ask him questions about school and his plans for life after graduation and discovered that he was pretty much on his own. Jayson responded to Marcus's mentorship and continued checking in regularly even after he was fully recovered. Just last year, Marcus had been invited to Jayson's wedding and his wife told him how much those conversations in the trainer's room had meant to her husband.

"Wow! That's awesome, man," Randal beamed. "That's a big deal. What would it take to make that kind of impact on other athletes?"

"I don't know." Marcus considered the question. "Probably just slowing down a little. I've gotten so efficient in my job that I'm not leaving any time to be effective. I'm so focused on checking the boxes of what each person needs for rehab that I don't think to ask them how they're doing in other areas of their lives."

"You know the pressure these kids are under to perform," Randal offered. "I wonder if their injury might be a chance for them to slow down long enough to think about some bigger, longer lasting things. And if you might be the one to ask those questions."

If you're not familiar with it, Russell Conwell's 1915 speech "Acres of Diamonds" was an inspiring call to Americans to begin working toward their dream right where they were because they were standing on untold riches. Instead of being tempted to move to another state or get another degree or take another job, he believed that any situation has potential benefit if we will put our proverbial shovels in the ground.

Backed by that same belief, I contend that **you can find increased fulfillment in your current job**. In fact, in my coaching program I guarantee it!

But it will take some work. Not the backbreaking work of mining for diamonds, but the time and effort required to put aside the old way of looking at your job and your employer and to put on the new lenses of your Career Factors. Let those with eyes to see...

This chapter is largely an opportunity for you to brainstorm different ways you can find career satisfaction in your current role. I can't be there beside you for this part, which is why it's so important that you realize that no one else can make you happy in your job but you. But that's also the exciting part; once you own it, you can pass it on. (More on that in the last chapter.)

On the following pages, I invite you to focus on your top two or three Career Factors and begin to identify ways you can meet the unique definitions that you laid out in chapter 5. Then pick one of the Career Factors and focus on increasing your internally-derived satisfaction for three weeks. This will take a little time, but choosing one factor and sticking with it for a while is the only way to change your focus.

Remember to start with small goals, especially by recalling what already exists at work that you may have forgotten about or neglected. Don't hesitate to ask someone else at work, even if you don't explain why you're inquiring.

And celebrate small wins. As I often say, "What you appreciate appreciates!" meaning that what you're grateful for usually ends up becoming more valuable to you.

After you finish your exploration of your first Career Factor, begin exploring opportunities to experience your second and then third Career Factor in the following weeks. You'll likely find that you can keep much of your top Career Factor while layering your second and third, empowering you to enjoy elements of your job—after all, no job is perfect—throughout each week.

Today's date: _____

My #1 Career Factor: _____

How I can experience more of it in my current role:

_____

_____

_____

_____

_____

_____

_____

_____

_____

_____

_____

_____

_____

_____

Today's date: _____

My #2 Career Factor: _____

How I can experience more of it in my current role:

_____

_____

_____

_____

_____

_____

_____

_____

_____

_____

_____

_____

_____

Today's date: _____

My #3 Career Factor: _____

How I can experience more of it in my current role:

_____

_____

_____

_____

_____

_____

_____

_____

_____

_____

_____

_____

_____

CHAPTER 8

Sharing The Wealth:
Helping others find fulfilling careers

"When you learn, teach.
When you get, give."
— Maya Angelou

—

thecareerfactors.com

"Knock knock!"

Fran looked up from the sea of papers on her desk to see Marcus at her door.

"Good morning, Marcus. This is unexpected. What can I do for you?"

"I was just in the neighborhood talking to Mika about Volunteer Day and I wanted to run an idea by you," Marcus replied.

"I'm all ears, and I'm glad you stopped by. I meant to follow up with you after our last conversation, but I've been swamped. Are you still considering leaving us?"

Marcus paused. "I'm not, despite how I felt after we last met. Actually, I've done a lot of thinking about my job and what I want from it. And I think I figured out what it will take to make me happy at work."

"That's great news, Marcus! I'm very pleased to hear that." And she seemed genuine.

"Thanks. But even more to the point, I may have stumbled upon a different way to think about work that we might be able to use to help a lot of people in the company enjoy their jobs more."

"Very interesting, Marcus. What do you have in mind?"

Marcus explained the Career Factors and how each person's awareness of their own combination along with the empowerment to find it in their current roles could increase productivity, improve company culture, and reduce turnover.

Fran was receptive to the idea but wanted to test it on a small group of people before presenting it to the executive team as a company-wide initiative. She suggested that Marcus meet with a few people who had given their notice as part of their exit interview. Marcus was excited to share his newfound perspective on career satisfaction, especially when he discovered that one of his team members had just submitted her letter of resignation.

Over the following months, Fran set up lunch appointments for Marcus with certain outgoing employees, and Marcus taught them about the Career Factors and learned more about what was—and wasn't—working to motivate employees at his company. He eventually compiled a list of recommendations that he and Fran brought to the leadership as part of a six-month plan to improve engagement and increase retention.

While the corporate program was well received, Marcus noticed that it was one-on-one interactions that created the greatest improvement in a person's career satisfaction. Most surprising—and enjoyable-- as he shared the Career Factors with others, he continued to refine and understand what made him happy at work. And that made all the difference.

As we reach the end of Marcus's journey, I hope you've been encouraged in a few ways. For one, I hope that you have a better understanding of what motivates you at work, whatever work looks like to you. I also want you to feel empowered by the idea that you have some control over your career satisfaction, even if only in small ways. Start small; your agency will grow as you use it.

Most of all, now that know about the Career Factors, I hope you'll share them with others, giving them a perspective about work that I know I didn't have when I initially chose my career and even two decades into working. You can share this approach to work in a few ways:

Give someone this book: If you've gleaned something valuable from *The Career Factors*, I encourage you to share it with someone else. You can find the book in all its forms at thecareerfactors.com.

Start a book study at work: You probably know a few people at work who want their careers to be more fulfilling but who don't have the tools to make it happen. Commit one lunch hour per week for a month to discuss what you're learning and help each other complete the lessons in chapters 5-7. Sometimes we need someone near us to help us see what's right in front of us.

Offer to be a mentor to new hires: Few factors matter more to an employee than the onboarding process and the first year, and often the HR department is overwhelmed with the demands of hiring, professional development, and workplace safety to mentor each new hire in the way they want. Volunteering to participate—or even create—a mentorship program is a powerful way to help shape the careers of those beginning their journey and perhaps rejuvenate those who have a few years under their belts already. Selfishly, it's a great way to make sure that your co-workers enjoy their jobs, too. It's always more fun to work with people who like their job!

Become a Career Factors coach: If the ideas and activities in this book resonate with you, you might consider being a Career Factors coach! We empower and equip individuals who are passionate about helping people of all ages (students, employees, and retirees) find rewarding work in their current and future roles. You can learn more about becoming a certified Career Factors coach at thecareerfactors.com.

However you use the Career Factors in your life, I hope that you'll create a rewarding career and a fulfilling life. Life's too short to be miserable at work.

All the best,
Sam

ACKNOWLEDGEMENTS

I was inspired by reading *How Will You Measure Your Life?* by Clayton Christensen, James Allworth, and Karen Dillon, particularly their insights on the research mentioned throughout this book. I highly recommend reading it once a year to keep your life in perspective.

I couldn't have made *The Career Factors* into what it is without the help of these friends in particular:

Dr. Bryan Hendley for writing the foreword and helping me build The Career Factors coaching program.

Chris Render for providing feedback on the assessments and co-creating The Career Factors for Students.

Deborah Nowe for the visual of the combination lock and for being everyone's favorite.

Dr. Margy Jones-Carey for the nudges I needed along the way.

Leigh Anne Lewis for copyediting the book like a mother.

Tyler House for being one of my first Career Factors guinea pigs and for providing valuable feedback about the coaching program and this book.

Zach Lush for pushing me to write "The Engagement Dilemma," which pushed me to transform The Career Factors from a good idea into one that I can share with others.

The rest of my True North mastermind: Paul Edwards, Raul Figueroa, Scott Hooper, Steve Kinsley, Clarence Montgomery. Jeff Ristine, Chad Stokes, Gary Wilburs, and Chuck Wood for their feedback on the book and their encouragement along my own career journey.

Above all, I'm grateful to God, whose gift of vocation often shows up in our careers.

ABOUT THE AUTHOR

Sam Feeney is the founder of the Career Factors and the creator of The Career Factors assessments. His work with students, adults, and companies is a continued attempt to help people live meaningful lives by finding fulfilling careers.

You can find out more about Sam, including opportunities for speaking and coaching at SamFeeney.com.